Words by Logan Thatcher

Copyright © 2020 Ted Satterfield

ISBN: 9781736175941

GRADUATION GIFT SERIES

Good Gift Books
and Merchandise™

Note from the Author

I'll share something with you that I'm often reluctant to share with other people: I love attending graduation ceremonies. Sure, they're often held in physically uncomfortable settings, and commencement speakers can be downright long-winded, but still, I love them. We celebrate achievements all the time in our society, but graduations are unique in their pageantry and formal celebration. It's a beautiful thing, and I honestly wish we had additional celebrations like this in our lives.

Graduations are still different than other achievements in life. It's not just the celebration of an accomplishment, but an acknowledgment of an abrupt ending to a significant phase of one's life. This is exciting, but it's also kind of like whiplash. The ending is jarring, leaving the graduate rather disoriented. But out of that disorientation, we see the beautiful beginning of an entirely different phase of life. The graduation ceremony is the recognition of the individuals who are, for just a brief moment, suspended between these two phases of life.

It's with this understanding that I approached this verse of appreciation for graduates. During a graduation ceremony, every person forced to wear matching robes and impractical hats is caught in a moment between two phases of life, but then that moment is over in a blink, and everyone goes back to normal. I like to think about this when I attend graduation ceremonies. There are no other moments quite like it, and for all of the graduates receiving this book, I hope this book helps you commemorate this brief and very special moment in your life.

Congratulations!

— Logan Thatcher

If a rumor
I heard,
in fact,
is true ...

A

congratulations,

to someone,

is due.

For a graduate
has made it
through ...

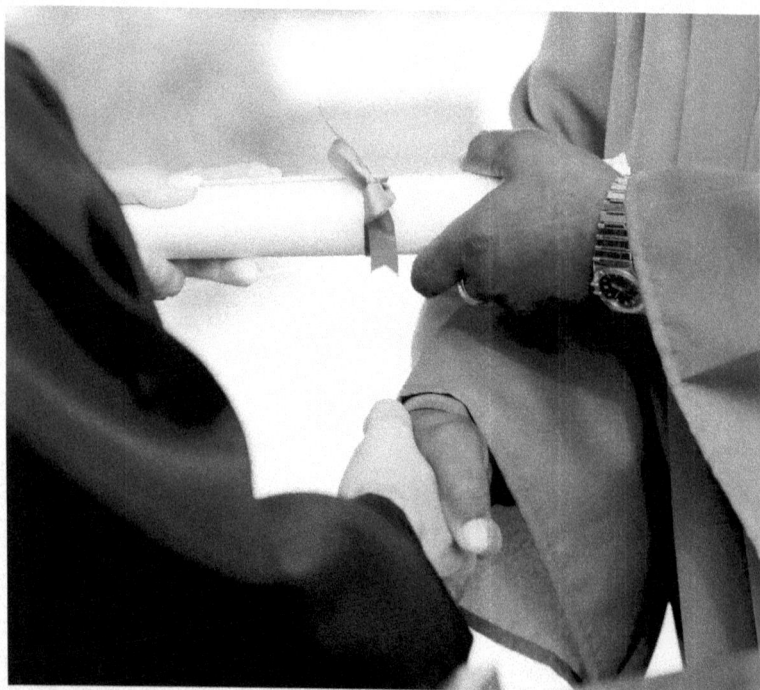

Rumor is,
that graduate,
is you.

So much hard
work, how comes
to an end ...

Things will now change; I won't pretend.

The first thing
to you that I'd
recommend ...

Is to celebrate,
at least for the
full weekend.

Take some time
to reflect on
all that you've
gained ...

Things that were lost, and things that remained.

That which you didn't know, that's how been explained ...

What you struggled to grasp, but

how is ingrained.

All you've acquired, while pursuing this dream ...

Learning so
much,
more than it
might seem.

Surely, you've learned how to work in a team...

And you
know how
to make
an effective
meme.

Frivolous Lawsuit

* Disclaimer: Please do not take the above image as an "effective meme." Doing so could lead to further creation of terrible memes, which is already rampant on social media.

You learned

many

different

ways

to think ...

When adversity comes, you rise, don't shrink.

You now have
a sense that
life goes
in a blink ...

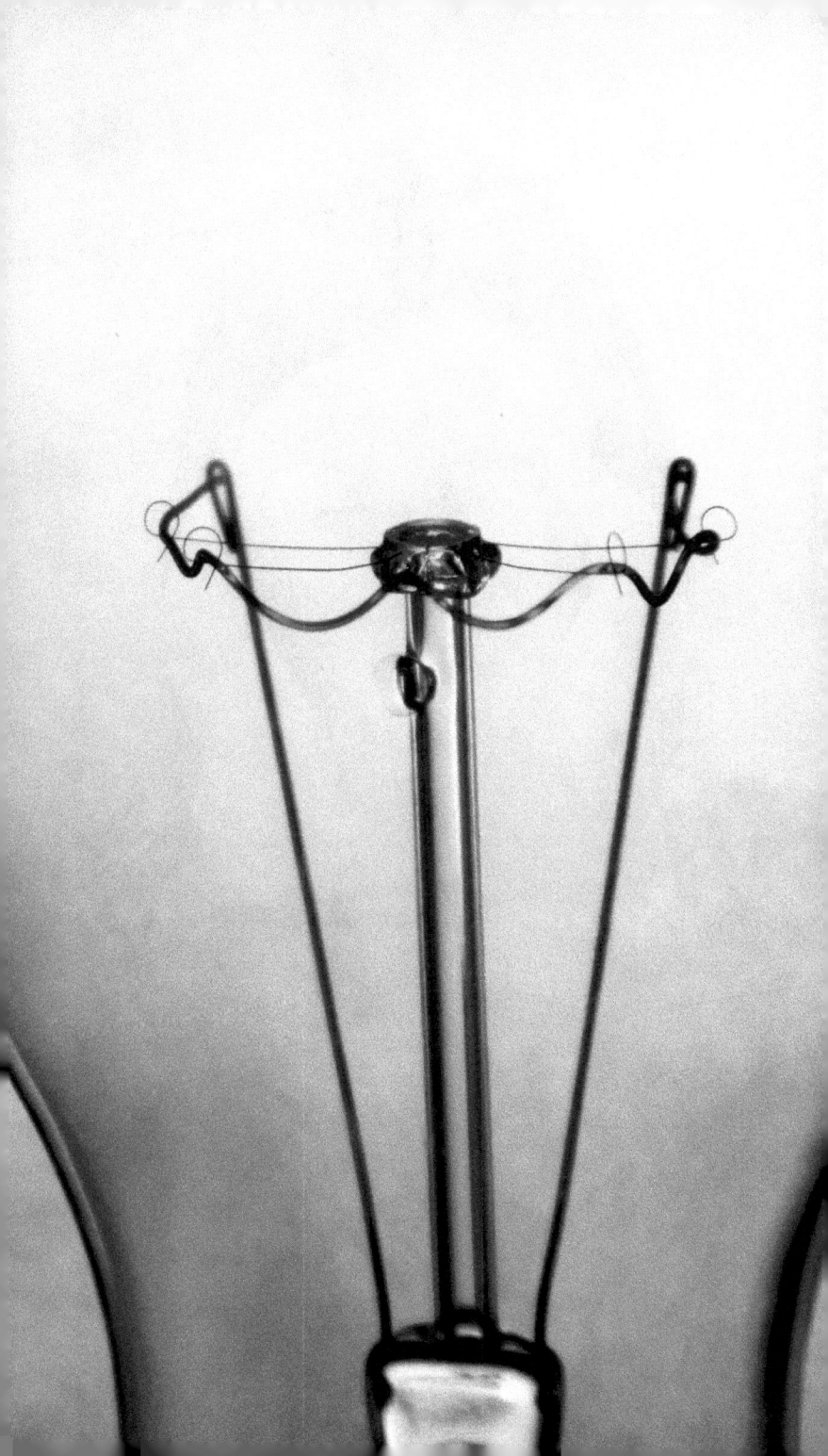

And how to avoid getting sick if you decide to drink.

You know
when to
read, and
when you
can skim ...

How to boost your mood when things look quite dim.

The best time
of day to go
hit the gym ...

When to use

a word,

or its

synonym.

Ones like you,
so smart and
clever ...

The world needs you more than ever.

You know
what
you like,
however ...

It's typically good to never say never.

As you

embark

on this

adventure

new ...

And show us

all what you

can do.

Just stick to
what you know
is true ...

And always
listen to
other points
of view.

The road
ahead, I know,
might seem
scary ...

Things might
go smooth;
things might
get hairy.

Bad times are
typically just
temporary ...

And some
things we
fear are only
imaginary.

When
adversity
comes, just
think of this
time ...

You're on top of the mountain you set out to climb.

Pay attention
to
others, and
if there's
downtime ...

Maybe pen
them note, or
just a nice
rhyme.

But, turning
back to the
moment at
hand ...

For this very
moment is
certainly
grand.

Back to
the rumor
spreading
across the
land ...

That
someone has
graduated,
I understand.

If this rumor
I heard,
in fact, is
true ...

That someone graduated, and made it through.

And if that
someone,
in fact, is
you:

A happy graduation, to you, is due!

Now as it's
time for me to
depart ...

I'll leave this
message from
my heart:

The end of this verse will be just like its start, as I proudly proclaim:

You're

Officially

Smart!

Congratulations
to all the
graduates
out there!!!

We hope you've enjoyed your copy of
"You're Officially Smart".

Good Gift Books
and Merchandise™

If you liked this book, you might like something else in Good Gift Books' Book-Length Greeting Card series. Available on Amazon.

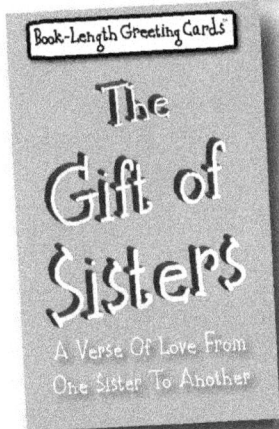

www.ingramcontent.com/pod-product-compliance
Lightning Source LLC
Chambersburg PA
CBHW071904020426
42331CB00010B/2666